I0473772

Retail Sales
&
Customer
Service

– Volume 2

CARLO G SANTORO

Copyright © 2012 Carlo G Santoro

All rights reserved.

ISBN: 1478251441
ISBN-13: 9781478251446

DEDICATION

This book is dedicated to all the future happy customers that are going to buy from you!

CONTENTS

ACKNOWLEDGMENTS

This book came about from years of watching and working with amazing retailers and inspiring people.....Thank you for all the knowledge you imparted.

I thank Sandy Newman for all her hard work and support in putting this book together.

I also thank my family: Debra, Silvia and Romeo.

FORWARD

Ok. Now that you've been introduced to the basic principles associated with a role in retail sales and customer service in Volume 1, you are ready to move onto Volume 2: Performing Retail Sales & Customer Service.

Ideally recommended to be read at the completion of Volume 1 to give a full & complete understanding of a retail sales and customer service role, this volume is also ideal as a 'refresher' for mature staff returning the workforce.

The chapters in this volume will serve to demonstrate the basic principles in various sales techniques, outlining why a particular method is used and how this is advantageous in a selling environment.

Basic procedures such as greetings, asking open and closed questions, and explaining features and benefits are discussed; working through the sales process in a logical manner to include closing the sale. Advanced techniques such as value-add-selling and positive pitching are also explained with examples, together with topics including, complaints handling, shop lifting and store security.

A comprehensive chapter on the Point of Sale (POS) area is included, with a fundamental coverage on POS equipment found in the retail workplace, to help make sure that you will have a really good understanding of the environment in which you are working.

Let's get to it!

CARLO G SANTORO

CARLO G SANTORO

VOLUME 2: PERFORMING RETAIL SALES & CUSTOMER SERVICE

CARLO G SANTORO

11. GREETINGS

"With businesses, you go to the same places because you like the service, you like the people and they take care of you. They greet you with a smile. That's how people want to be treated, with respect. That's what I tell my employees... customer service is very important."

Magic Johnson - African American businessman, entrepreneur and returned NBA basketball player

Creating a Positive Shopping Experience for Customers

Now that we have looked at some of the principles behind the importance of good customer service, sales, and how to prepare and present yourself each day in you role as a salesperson, it's time to move onto the shop floor. In this chapter, we will look at the key aspects of greeting your customers professionally. The greeting is the initial contact with a customer. This is where the first impression of you, as a retail salesperson, is made. When done properly, your greeting will outline how the customers' shopping experience will be.

Timely Greeting

There are many ways to greet a customer. This can be as simple as saying "hello". It is important, however, that you greet every customer no longer than within one minute of them entering the store. This will show the customer that you are aware they are in the store. If a customer is not greeted within one minute, the chance of them walking out of your store without buying increases significantly.

Remember too, that everyone's perception of time can vary. One minute may seem very short to you, but it could appear to be a long time in a customer's mind, particularly if they are expecting to be greeted immediately upon entering the store. Take no longer than one minute to greet your customer, but doing so in less than one minute is also quite acceptable.

In addition, if there are other salespeople on the floor with you, don't assume that they will have greeted a new customer entering the store and that if so, it is safe for you to then ignore them. A second "hello" from you will not be seen as offensive by the customer. If neither of you greet the customer, however, as you each assumed that the other one had, the customer will end up without any greeting at all, which leaves a poor impression. If you are not sure if another team member may have already greeted the customer, then at least a smile from you is better than nothing at all.

There are many ways in which you can greet a customer. No matter how you choose to greet a customer, you must ensure that you are professional and show that you are willing to assist them.

Greeting a Customer While Serving Another Customer

There will be times when a customer walks into your store while you are assisting another customer. It is still crucial that you greet these customers within one minute. This is best done by simply by acknowledging that they are there and telling them that you will be with them momentarily. Once again, this shows the customer that you are aware of their presence and they will feel welcome.

Greeting a Regular Customer

Repeat or regular customers will become obvious to you over time. The fact that they are revisiting your store more than likely means that they were previously satisfied with a product or service that they obtained from you, and the level of customer service that they received. They still need to be greeted warmly and made to feel extremely welcome from the minute that they enter the store. Remember, they have come back to hopefully purchase again, and you want to ensure that this continues.

Greet regular customers by name, if you know it. Sometimes, shaking their hand may also be appropriate. Everyone likes to be made to feel special, and using a customer's name in your greeting shows that you remember them from a previous occasion and are demonstrates a degree of rapport that you have built with them, which is extremely important in terms of repeat business.

Your Position in the Store

After greeting a customer, you must ensure that you do not stay behind the counter. This is to show the customer that you are happy to be helping them. Under no circumstance is "back of house" work more important than customer service. If a customer enters your store, they are your number one priority. This will also help with loss prevention as you are focusing on what is happening within your store, not behind it.

*Remember: *First* impressions *last.*

"We see our customers as invited guests to a party, and we are the hosts. It's our job every day to make every important aspect of the customer experience a little bit better."

Jeff Bezos - Founder of the popular online book store Amazon.com.

Examples of appropriate greetings:

"Hello. How are you? Is there something I can help you with?"

"Hi. My name is _____. Can I give you a hand with something?

"Hello. I will be with you in just a moment."

"Hello. Are you looking for something in particular?

Appropriate greetings while serving another customer:

"Hello. I will be with you in just a moment."

"Hi. I won't be a sec."

"Hello. I'll be with you as soon as I can."

Appropriate greetings for repeat or regular customers:

"Hello Mr Smith. How are you?"

"Hi Mrs Johnson. How can I help you today?"

"Mr Delaney? Nice to see you again. What can I do for you today?"

12. DISCOVERY

"You will make more friends in a week by getting yourself interested in other people than you can in a year by trying to get other people interested in you."

Arnold Bennett – British novelist

The Importance of 'Discovery'

To be a successful salesperson, you must ensure that you gather as much information as possible, to be able to fulfill your customers' needs. This process is called *'discovery'*.

Discovery is used to get your customer talking. The more your customer talks to you, the more information you can gather. Discovery is done simply by asking a mix of open and closed questions. These questions will help you to gain information to be able to offer the correct solution the first time.

The number of questions you ask and the length of time spent on discovery may be dependent upon the product or service you are selling. For example, technical products or services may initiate a more factual discussion with a customer, whereas fashion items or homewares may include more questions around lifestyle. The whole point of the conversation is to lead you back to the product - gathering helpful information along the way about your customer's needs - and come to a close.

Without discovery, the solutions you offer your customers may not be exactly what they need, or want. Discovery will help you to paint a picture of your customer's lifestyle, work and family commitments. These three areas can all produce *'triggers'* which may assist you to sell. (We will look at triggers shortly).

The Funnel Technique

Discovery is done by asking a mix of open and closed questions. These questions are put together using a process called *'The Funnel Technique.'*

If you consider the design of a funnel, the liquid enters the most open part of the funnel before passing through the narrow end, to pour out and create the desired result. Discovery is done in a very similar way. Your initial questions should be primarily open questions, followed by a few closed questions. The desired solution can then be created.

Open Questions

Open questions are questions which help to get the customer talking. These questions will require an answer of more than just a simple "*yes*" or "*no*". Open questions tend to start with words such as **who, what, when, where, why** and **how**.

These questions will help you to paint a picture of the customer's work life, lifestyle and family life, as well as physical and emotional needs. Asking open questions gives you the chance to hear 'triggers' from your customers.

Some examples of open questions are:

"What do you do for work?"

"What are your hobbies?"

"Who are you purchasing for?"

"What are the main uses for this product/service?"

"How much do you normally spend on this sort of product/service?"

Closed Questions

Closed questions are questions that will have a limited answer. The answer to a closed question will usually be either *"yes"* or *"no"*. Closed questions are used to narrow down the answers to your open questions. When you ask open questions, you will need to confirm the answers with closed questions. Closed questions tend to start with the words **have, will, do, is, does, did** and **can**.

Some examples of closed questions are:

"Do you have any other product/service like this?"

"Do you travel a lot?"

"Will you be using this product/service frequently?"

"Have you heard about this product/service before?"

"Did you have a particular brand in mind?"

"Can you use something like this at home?"

Remember, using discovery will not only help you to complete the initial customer enquiry but will also give you the chance to value-add, up-sell and cross-sell.

Identifying Triggers

Triggers are comments or statements made by a customer, which may lead to further sales opportunities. You may come across triggers at any time during the sales process, however most triggers evolve during the discovery process.

If you pick up on triggers and relay that back to the customer by offering solutions around the trigger, you will show the customer that you have been paying attention to what they have been saying. This will help to build trust.

A trigger can be any sort of statement. It could be a statement made about work, lifestyle and family, physical or emotional needs. A trigger will also help to paint a picture of the needs of the customer.

Some examples of triggers are:

"It's mostly for use downstairs, 'though sometimes the guest room upstairs also needs cleaning"

"I'll be the main one using it, but I guess my kids will want to have a go too"

"I usually travel light and prefer a smaller case, but sometimes I need to take extra things for an extended stay"

In the first example, during a discussion with a customer about a vacuum cleaner, a trigger is revealed in the fact that occasionally it will be required for use upstairs. This gives the salesperson the opportunity to suggest a selection of lighter weight models to choose from.

The salesperson assisting the customer with the suitcase in the last example, could suggest a model that is compact but has a zip-out extension when required to accommodate extra items.

Using Triggers When Selling

As well as helping to pinpoint the best solution for your customer, picking up on triggers can also lead to *value-add-selling*, *up-selling* or *cross-selling*, where an additional item, higher priced item or slightly different item to what the customer first intended to buy may be sold to the customer as the result of the triggers revealed during discovery. We will look at each of these selling techniques in more detail in *Chapter 17 – Additional Selling Techniques*.

"When I'm under the gun and I've got pressure on me, I don't panic. I look for the right solution, and then I go for it."

Magic Johnson - African American businessman, entrepreneur and returned NBA basketball player

An example of Discovery using the Funnel Technique:

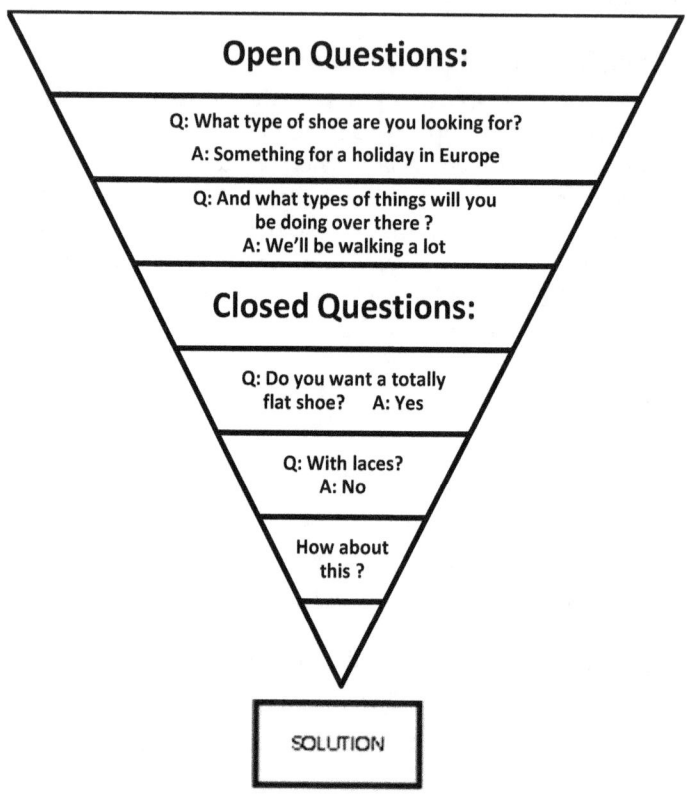

13. OFFERING THE SOLUTION

"Customers today want the very most and the very best for the very least amount of money, and on the best terms. Only the individuals and companies that provide absolutely excellent products and services at absolutely excellent prices will survive."

Brian Tracy - Self-help author and business coach

What is a Solution?

Ideally, we would like to be able to provide the customer with exactly what they are looking for. Whether it's a gift for a friend who has everything, a new computer with state of the art capabilities or simply a comfortable pair of walking shoes for an up and coming holiday, the customer has a need and, as sales people, we would like to fulfill it and make a sale. In order to do this, we need to be sure that we have fully understood what the customer wants or needs and come up with a suitable solution to offer them.

Matching Your Solution to the Information Gathered During Discovery

After asking appropriate discovery questions, you should have collected the correct information to suggest a suitable product or service. This is called *offering a solution*. The solution should always match the needs of the customer. Occasionally, it may be appropriate to offer the customer something slightly different to what they first had in mind, but this should not be your first course of action.

Offering Solutions

Generally, it is important that you only offer one or two suitable solutions to the customer. If you offer more than this to the customer, you may find that you will give them too much to think about and they may not buy anything on that particular occasion. If the discovery process is done properly, using the 'Funnel Technique', you will usually be left with one or maybe two solutions for the customer that best suits their needs.

Exceptions

Whilst offering only one or two solutions has the advantage of not confusing your customer, depending upon the situation, it may be more appropriate to offer more than this. This is where your skills as a salesperson and the information that you gathered during discovery will help you decide the best course of action to take.

At times, too, the 'Funnel Technique' could break down as the customer changes their mind along the way. They may start out thinking that they want one particular thing – an umbrella, for example – and end up realising that their specific needs to best suit their lifestyle dictate something different – in this instance, a raincoat.

There will also be times when we can't provide an exact solution or a direct solution, but we can provide the customer with the awareness of what we can offer that still relates to the customer's needs. This may not be a direct solution at the onset, but sometimes, will lead to a sale just the same.

For example, a female customer may want a red dress for a party. Your store may not have any red dresses in her size. You could suggest that perhaps a black one with red accessories could still fulfill her needs and actually be more versatile as she will then have a great black dress to wear for many other occasions. Again, this is where your skills as a salesperson will come into play and have a direct impact on the success (or failure) of your sale.

Explaining Features & Benefits

When offering a solution to your customer, it is crucial that you explain the key *features* and *benefits* of the product or service you are offering. Remember that **features** are the actual functions or capabilities that the product or service has, and the **benefits** are how these can help the customer. Highlighting the features and benefits – especially those that are relevant to the customer's needs - will qualify your suggested solution. If this is done, you usually prevent your customer from raising objection to your solution and more often than not, it will lead to a successful sale. Features & Benefits are explained in more detail in the next chapter – *Creating Interest with Features & Benefits*.

Take Control of the Conversation

When offering the solution, unlike discovery, you must take control of the conversation. This is to give you the chance to explain the product or service in detail and ensure the customer is given all the relevant and important information about the product or service that they are considering. While taking control of the conversation, you must also ensure that you are prepared to answer any questions from your customer.

Balance

Taking control of the conversation in this way requires a degree of skill in that there must also be *balance*. Taking control does not mean being too overbearing. Your conversation should be informative and relevant, whilst at the same time answering any questions that the customer may raise. It is your job to ensure that the conversation doesn't get too off track with side issues. If this occurs, as a professional salesperson, you should be able to steer them back on track to the topic at hand.

Space

It is also important to keep track of time and remember that there may be other customers who also need your assistance. Most customers appreciate being given a bit of space to think about your solution on their own, without you being right next to them. This prevents them feeling pressured into buying or being put on the spot and made to feel uncomfortable about making a quick decision. It is quite acceptable to politely ask their permission to go away momentarily and give them a few minutes to think. This will also give you the opportunity to start up a conversation with other customers, who may be waiting, whilst not forgetting, however, that your first customer should be rejoined in a few moments in order for you to hopefully close the sale.

Always Be Closing (ABC)

During the process of offering the solution, you must always acknowledge that the customer understands what you are saying. This is done by using the *ABC process*. This stands for *Always Be Closing*. ABC is done by asking questions such as *"How does that sound?"* or *"Does that sound ok?"*

When we follow the ABC process, we ensure that we gain acceptance from the customer. The more that we hear the customer say "Yes" during the ABC process, the less likely the customer will say "No" at the end. This will also help prevent the customer from presenting us with objections. This process is covered in more detail later.

"The difference between a mountain and a molehill is your perspective."

<u>Al Neuharth</u> – American businessman, author and columnist

CARLO G SANTORO

14. CREATING INTEREST WITH FEATURES & BENEFITS

"You are surrounded by simple, obvious solutions that can dramatically increase your income, power, influence and success. The problem is, you just don't see them."

Jay Abraham – Business growth strategist and author

What is Creating Interest & Acceptance (CIA)?

Creating interest and acceptance (CIA) is a key factor in the sales process. This is where you will help your customers to become interested in talking to you about the products or services you are selling. CIA will also gain you acceptance to allow you to continue to make your sale.

The Importance of Creating Interest & Acceptance

CIA is important, as your customer needs to be interested in talking and listening to you. If a customer loses interest, they are not likely to engage in conversation with you. This means you will have less or no chance of making a successful sale.

How to Create Interest & Acceptance

- To create **interest**, you will need to make yourself and the products and services you are selling appeal to your customer.

This is done by using several techniques:

➢ Using appealing words

➢ Explaining features & benefits

➢ Using active listening skills

We will look at each of these techniques in more detail shortly.

- To gain **acceptance**, you will need to ask the customer a simple question. The question you ask is simply to gain acceptance to continue with your sale.

Some examples of questions to gain acceptance from your customer are:

"How does that free offer sound?"

"Would you like me to show you how you can save money?"

"Would you like me to show you how I can add value to your existing service?"

These questions, and more, will assist you in gaining acceptance from your customer to continue with your sale. They will show the customer that you are offering to save them money, give them value for money, or better still, give them additional items free !

Appealing Words

Appealing words are words which will stand out to your customers and attract their attention. Words such as **free**, and **bonus** are some examples of appealing words. Others could include:

- save

- extra

- complimentary

- time saving

- value

These appealing words, especially when used in an opening sentence, will generate interest from your customer. They will show your customer that you are offering a solution that may benefit them and their needs.

Features & Benefits

Customer needs are categorised into two separate types. They are: *physical* and *emotional*. A customer will buy based on emotional needs but the physical/logical need is what triggers the emotion. The physical and emotional needs are met by using **features** and **benefits**. Features and benefits are the key selling points when explaining a product or service to your customer. They will assist in matching the correct solution to your customer's needs.

FEATURES

Features are the **components** included in a product or service. They are **physical** services, functions or accessories that will benefit the customer and their physical needs. For example, when selling a mobile phone, the features could be: a camera, GPS, internet facilities, a touch screen and video calling. If you are selling a car, the features could be: air conditioning, keyless entry, alloy wheels and ABS. A feature could also be that a product or service is less costly than expected. This is a physical attribute or inclusion in the product or service.

BENEFITS

A benefit is the **advantage** that comes with using the feature. Benefits will assist in fulfilling your customer's emotional needs. In the mobile phone example above, the inclusion of a camera is a physical feature which will benefit your customer by enabling them to take pictures and remember moments from their past. The benefit of a product or service being less costly is that the customer will have more money for the other important things in their life.

Promoting Features with Benefits

Promoting features & benefits will also help create interest in your customer. Every time we promote a **feature**, we must also ensure we promote the **benefit**. This is to ensure we help trigger the customer's emotional needs. If you do not promote the benefit, the initial response from the customer may be *"So what?"* By promoting the benefit of a feature, you reduce the risk of facing objections.

Some products or services may be loaded with features and benefits and others not so much, which may make your job appear difficult. A good salesperson, however, will always be able to find some features and associated benefits to point out to their customer. This is where good product knowledge is essential.

Using Active Listening Skills

Using active listening skills is essential when trying to create interest and acceptance from your customer. Active listening is done by using specific actions for specific associated reasons.

Active listening shows your customer respect, and will also enable you to correctly interpret all the information that they are giving you, enabling you to offer the correct solution to suit their needs.

Using the Funnel Technique

As we have seen in Chapter 12, the 'Funnel Technique' is a process used to help you establish the correct solution to offer to your customer to fulfill their needs. Active listening skills are a vital part of this process, as they ensure that you are taking in and correctly interpreting what your customer is saying to you about what their particular needs are.

If you are using active listening skills throughout the 'funnel technique' process, you will have a much better chance at arriving at the correct and best solution for your customer in your initial conversation.

Practice active listening skills with your team mates, or even your friends. You will be amazed at how your communication skills will be dramatically improved and the benefits that this will bring!

"The difference between a successful person and others is not a lack of strength, not a lack of knowledge, but rather a lack of will."

Vincent T. Lombardi - Renowned American football coach

Active Listening is done by the following actions for the following reasons:

ACTION	REASON
❖ Using and maintaining eye contact with your customer	❖ Shows your customer respect
❖ Nodding of your head	❖ Shows agreement and comprehension of what your customer is saying
❖ Repeating back points that were made by the customer	❖ Shows that you were listening intently and have comprehended what your customer said
❖ Complete concentration on what customer is asking for	❖ Shows that you are completely engaged with your customer and not distracted
❖ Asking relevant questions back to the customer	❖ Shows that you are following what they are saying, but you may need some further clarification on some points to be sure that you have understood correctly
❖ Never interrupting the customer while they are speaking – always wait until they finish	❖ Shows respect to your customer and good manners
❖ Using positive and open body language	❖ Shows that you are interested in what they have to say and are open to listening to them

15. OVERCOMING OBJECTIONS

"Obstacles are necessary for success because in selling, as in all careers of importance, victory comes only after many struggles and countless defeats."

Og (Augustine) Mandino - American Salesman and best-selling author of motivational sales books

What is an Objection?

Your biggest obstacles when selling are *customer objections*. Customer objections are negative feelings or attitude towards the solution you offer. An objection can also include confusion, where your customer is unsure whether to go ahead with the purchase or not, or it can be an outright objection with your customer simply saying "no". As a salesperson, you must try to prevent or overcome objections. This is to ensure that you secure the sale while also making the customer feel more comfortable about their purchase.

Reasons for Objections

There are many reasons why a customer might present

objections to the solution that you are offering them. Some of these could include price, brand, physical factors, circumstances, on-going associated costs or country of origin. Some customers may present several objections to a solution you are offering, while other customers may not present any at all. If you are presented with objections by your customer, it is best to listen clearly to what the customer is saying and find and isolate the objection raised, in order to deal with it.

Some reasons for objections from customers could be:

❖ Price	➢ it is above their intended spending amount
❖ Brand	➢ they don't like that brand; they have had problems with it before
❖ Physical factors	➢ it is simply too big, too small or the wrong shape etc to meet their needs
❖ Research mode only	➢ the customer is not ready to buy yet, but is researching what is available
❖ Circumstances	➢ they are in a hurry today or have children with them and can't think properly
❖ Ongoing costs	➢ the item requires dry cleaning or uses consumables which will equate to more costs in the future
❖ Country of origin	➢ some customers will only buy products made in their particular country and may reject an imported item

Preventing Objections

Preventing objections can be as simple as explaining the features and benefits of your solution and matching these features and benefits to your customer's needs (uncovered during the 'discovery' process). The closer that you match your solution to the customer's specific needs, the less likely it is that they will present an objection. It is not always possible, however, to completely prevent objections. If your customer does present an objection, you will then need to try to overcome it.

Overcoming Objections

Objections can be overcome by using many different processes. Sometimes it's just a matter of offering a similar product or service in a different price point, different size or different style. At other times, maybe a different quality or a product that fits with the customer's preference on country of origin. If a customer is in a hurry or in research mode, giving them some brochures or information to take home and read at their leisure is a good way to help overcome future objections on that particular product or service and may win you the sale later.

Other useful processes to help overcome objections include:

> 'Feel, Felt, Found'

> Asking more 'Discovery' questions

> More detailed features & benefits

Feel, Felt, Found

Feel, Felt, Found is a process used to describe how other customers have felt about the product or service you are offering. Customers are more likely to purchase if they know that other customers have been satisfied with the same purchase.

- **Feel** - the initial emotional state of the customer towards the product or service you are offering

- **Felt** - feelings that other customers may have had previously toward that same (or similar) product or service, which you have helped them overcome

- **Found** - final customer acceptance of the benefits of the product or service, from your assistance, communication and discovery process

An example of Feel, Felt, Found is:

*"I understand how you **feel** about the cost of this mobile phone plan. There have been other people who have **felt** that the cost may be a little too high. However, after learning that they will receive some free calls on their plan, effectively reducing home phone usage, they have **found** that they will actually be saving money."*

Ask More Discovery Questions

You may also need to ask more discovery questions to assist in overcoming objections. If you have not asked the correct questions initially, you may have overlooked the correct solution, effectively leaving yourself open for objections. If you are required to ask more discovery questions, you may end up offering another or slightly different solution to the first one. Sometimes, initially, the customer does not fully disclose exactly what they are looking for and it's only after an objection that the customer's specific needs become fully clear.

Asking more discovery questions can usually be done by recapping a little and then continuing on with the 'Funnel Technique' where you left off. Make sure that you take note of the reason that the customer has raised an objection to your first solution offered – was it because it was too big, too small, too expensive, not the right style etc and incorporate this into your continuation with the funnel technique. Doing this correctly should ensure that you are able to offer an alternative and suitable solution to your customer.

To reduce the chance of having to complete the whole sales process again, be sure to ask the right questions the first time to find out all of the information required to make a sale. Sometimes, too, the customer may have changed their mind along the way by the outcome of the discovery conversation or due to increased knowledge gained about the product or service. They may, therefore, drive the sale towards a different product or service as a solution, and sometimes without even realising it!

Explaining Features & Benefits in More Detail

Explaining features and benefits is generally used to prevent a customer raising objections, however, this may not always be the case. If your customer does not fully understand how the features will benefit them, they may not see how the solution you are offering is the right one for them. In this case, you may find that you need to explain the features and benefits again, or in more detail. In doing so, however, as always, you will need to ensure that you match the physical feature of your product or service on offer to the customer's needs that you uncovered during the discovery process.

In your recap of the features and benefits, start with the most relevant ones and make sure that your customer fully understands them. Sometimes it may be better to just review those in more detail, and leave other, irrelevant features or benefits for the moment, so as not to overwhelm your customer with too much repetitive information.

Using phrases like:

"Don't forget that this can............... "

"Did I show you how this ....?"

"I think this will really help you......... "

can help to make your recap a little less repetitive. Encourage your customer to ask questions too, to make sure that the fully understand exactly what you are trying to convey.

Always Be Closing (ABC)

Similarly to when you are offering the solution, during the objection handling process, it is helpful if you are using the *ABC process* – **Always be Closing**. As we saw in an earlier chapter, this process helps safeguard that the customer is understanding what you are saying. ABC is done by asking questions such as *"How does that sound?"* or *"Does that sound ok?"*.

To recap from before, when we follow the ABC process, we ensure that we gain acceptance from the customer. The more that we hear the customer say "Yes" during the ABC process, the less likely the customer will say "No" at the end. This will also help prevent the customer from presenting us with objections. This process is covered in more detail in *Chapter 16 – Closing the Sale.*

"There's no substitute for hard work."

Thomas Edison - American inventor & scientist

Other Useful Techniques

Even if you think that an objection is a flat out "*No*" for a particular sale, there are still things that you can do as a salesperson to maximise the potential for a sale with that customer at a future date. You can:

❖ *Remind the customer of who you are* - Take advantage of the opportunity to remind them of who you are by giving them a business card with the store phone number and your name and let them know that if there is any way that you can help them later, don't hesitate to call.

❖ *Get the customer's details* - So you can follow up on their objection or other queries that they might have had. This might involve a call to the manufacturer or discussions with your manager to answer anything that you can't help them with that day.

❖ *Highlight your business* - Remind them of things like the store opening hours, sister outlets (if a chain store), your 'no fuss' returns policy for change of mind etc. All these things help the customer feel that it is easy to do business with you and your store and will encourage them to come back again.

CARLO G SANTORO

16. CLOSING THE SALE

"People get caught up in wonderful, eye-catching pitches, but they don't do enough to close the deal. It's no good if you don't make the sale. Even if your foot is in the door or you bring someone into a conference room, you don't win the deal unless you actually get them to sign on the dotted line."

Donald Trump - Billionaire real estate developer

The Importance of Closing the Sale

Closing the sale is the quickest and most simple part of making a sale yet often the most mishandled. It is simply defined as *asking for the sale.*

Many people in a sales role do not close a sale properly. This is usually due to salespeople being too nervous or afraid to ask for the sale, for fear of hearing the word *"No"* from a customer. It is important to remember that as a salesperson, if you've done your job, it's quite ok to ask for the sale. If all the sales processes have been followed correctly, and you have offered the correct solution to the customer, there should be no reason for the customer to say *"No"*.

Always Be Closing (ABC)

As you have now learned, in the process of offering the solution or overcoming objections with your customer, using the ABC process will help ensure that we gain acceptance from them and encourage the customer to give us their consent to proceed. The more that we hear the customer say "*Yes*" during the ABC process, the less likely the customer will say "*No*" at the end. Using this technique towards the end of the conversation steers you nicely into closing the sale.

How to Close

Closing is done simply by inviting the customer to join you at your point of sale to process their order. This can be done by asking a question or making a statement. Often, value-add-selling* is done at this point as well.

As you are working through the sales process, if you can see that it is going well, your conversation with the customer should be heading towards closing the sale.

This can be done by using closing questions and statements such as:

"Would you like me to process this order for you now?"

"Would you like to take a seat while I process this order for you?"

"If you would like to take a seat, I will begin processing that for you now."

"Will that be all for you today, or can I help you with something else?"

Closing can also be combined with helping to make it easier for your customer to continue shopping and thereby possibly making additional purchases.

For example: *"I'll take these dresses to the counter for you while you continue looking."*

By asking these questions or making these statements, we gain acceptance from the customer to close the sale. This then prevents them from leaving the store without purchasing, allowing us to complete the successful transaction.

Opportunities with Closing

Closing can lead to opportunities to *value-add-sell* and *up-sell*, 'though it is important not to confuse or annoy the customer if you can see that they want to simply pay for their goods and leave. (We will look at value-add-selling and up-selling in the next chapter, Chapter 17)

When closing a sale, it is often appropriate to try to value-add or mention any special offers or incentives that might be particularly relevant to your customer. This should be done by way of just a quick mention at first, however, to gauge their initial reaction. If they show interest, it is safe to proceed with the pitch. If not, then perhaps hold off. Some customers will not want to hear a new sales pitch on something else when they are ready to pay for their current purchase and leave the store, whereas others will be happy to listen if it means that they will benefit by taking advantage of a promotion, entering a store competition or joining a VIP Club or loyalty program etc.

Failure to Close

Although closing a sale is a standard procedure and the ultimate goal for a salesperson, there will be times when you are not able to close the sale and this could be for various reasons. A lack of product knowledge will almost certainly lead to a failure to close, as the customer will find it difficult to have all their questions answered if you do not know the right information to deliver. A lack of product knowledge will also not help to persuade an indecisive customer to proceed with a purchase that they are deliberating on.

Some customers, too, although maybe sold on the idea of the purchase initially, simply are not ready to 'sign on the dotted line' right there and then. They may want to confer with a partner, or give it some more thought before proceeding. It is vital in situations like this not to railroad or try to bully the customer into proceeding. This is *not* an effective method of closing and will only serve to undermine your professionalism and credibility as a salesperson. The correct course of action in this case would be to offer the customer some more time to think about the purchase, or ask if there is anything else that you can do to assist them in conjunction with product or the purchase.

Different Strokes for Different Folks

Just as different staff members will have different personalities, you may find too, that they have slightly different styles when it comes to their selling techniques – particularly when closing. With different techniques, one or the other is not necessarily right or wrong, so long as the basic principles of sales and good customer service are adhered to. It is often a good idea to observe other team member's selling styles and compare them with your own. Maybe there is something you can learn?

"He who finds diamonds must grapple in mud and mire because diamonds are not found in polished stones. They are made."

Henry B. Wilson - American admiral and war veteran of WWI

Queue Busting

Queue Busting is a relatively new technological advancement in retail, entailing the use of a 'mobile checkout' by way of a handheld device, that a salesperson can use anywhere in the store.

Initially designed as a way to eliminate long checkout lines and increase customer satisfaction, 'queue busting' can be used as a way to help prevent losing sales that are already closed (but just not paid for yet), which could be jeopardised by the length of time the customer will need to wait in the queue to be served.

'Queue busting' is particularly useful in peak periods and particularly in larger stores, where queue time can become quite lengthy.

Depending on the item(s) intended for purchase, if a customer can be offered the option to conduct their transaction right then and there without even joining a queue to do so, many customers contemplating on whether or not to proceed with their purchase will find themselves saying "*Yes*" and thereby confirming that the sale is closed.

(So far, this method can only be used if the customer is paying by credit card).

CARLO G SANTORO

17. ADDITIONAL SELLING TECHNIQUES

"Business is not financial science, it's about trading... buying and selling. It's about creating a product or service so good that people will pay for it."

Anita Roddick – Founder of 'The Body Shop' chain of stores

Value-Add-Selling, Up-Selling & Cross-Selling

When selling to a customer, you may discover that they will have other needs to what they initially disclosed. To maximise your sales potential, while also meeting all of your customer's needs, you should try to *value-add*, *up-sell* and *cross-sell*.

There is a distinct difference between these three selling methods, but all are useful and powerful techniques that will usually result in higher returns for the business.

The Definition of Value-Add Selling

Value-add is defined as selling an *extra* product or service to your customer. We've all heard the commonly used phrase: *"Would you like fries with that?"*. This is an example of value-add selling, where the customer is offered the addition of French fries to go with his/her hamburger.

With value-add selling, your customer will come to your business with a specific need in mind, but you may discover that they have more than just that initial need and will happily buy an additional item that enhances or compliments the original item or service that they came in for or are in the process of buying.

When you value-add, you must always explain the features and benefits of the additional product or service. Your customer will want to know what the advantage is for them to spend the extra money.

Value-adding will also benefit your business with the sale of an additional item, but you must make sure the customer has a genuine need for the extra product or service before offering it. You must ensure that you are not leading them astray and selling them something that they don't need.

Some examples of value-add selling are:

- Selling shoe polish to a customer purchasing a new pair of boots

- Selling a carry case to a customer purchasing a laptop

- Selling a side salad to a customer ordering a meal in a restaurant

The Definition of Up-Selling

Up-selling is *increasing the value* of a product or service, as opposed to selling an additional product or service as with value-add selling. While this will usually come at a cost to your customer, it will often also be more beneficial, as they will usually be purchasing a higher grade product or service.

Up-selling is also beneficial to your business. If you up-sell from a $10 product or service to a $20 product or service, your business will generally make more money. You must always make sure, however, that if you up-sell, you are benefiting the customer and not just aiming for a higher priced sale.

To up-sell, again, you should always explain the advantage of the up-sell to the customer. If a customer is going to spend more money, they will want to know exactly how they will benefit. There is no point trying to up-sell if the customer will not gain from it. This will only create a sense of mistrust in the customer of you as a salesperson.

Some examples of up-selling are:

- Selling a brand name item to a customer thinking of purchasing a generic brand

- Selling a large size pizza to a customer originally ordering a medium for two people to share

- Selling a $35 hard cover book to a customer originally planning to purchase the $20 paperback version

The Definition of Cross-Selling

Cross-selling is *transitioning* from selling a product or service that the customer originally sought or asked for, to selling a slightly different product or service that better suits their needs. Usually, this transition will come about as a result of "discovery", or by picking up on "triggers" revealed during conversation with the customer.

For example, a customer at a car dealership may initially say he is interested in purchasing a four wheel drive vehicle, but he reveals that he pretty much never intends to actually take the vehicle off suburban streets and highways. An observant salesperson here would perhaps suggest a slightly different vehicle that has some similar features to the four wheel drive version that the customer was keen on, but is easier to manoeuvre and is more economical on fuel. The customer agrees that this second option is a much better solution for city driving and is happy to make the switch.

In some cases, cross-selling will also benefit the business more as it could carry a higher margin, earn a better rebate from a supplier, or simply be an item that of which there are plenty in stock and the business is keen to move.

Sometimes, however, cross-selling may result in selling the customer an item that carries a lower price tag than the original item sought, thereby generating a smaller sale and possibly less income for the business. If this new item, however, is the correct item to fully satisfy the customer's needs, then it is still far better to cross-sell to this item and give the customer exactly what they want. Your skills as a salesperson will come into play in situations like this, where it will be up to you to decide the best course of action to take.

Some examples of cross-selling are:

- Selling a raincoat to a customer asking for an umbrella

- Selling a laptop to a customer originally planning on a desktop

- Selling a docking station for an *i-pod* to a customer thinking of purchasing a portable stereo system

Identifying Opportunities

Depending on your retail business, there may be many different opportunities to value-add, up-sell or cross-sell. Opportunities can be anything from watching the customer moving through the store and observing what areas they are showing interest in, what they are looking at, picking up or what types of things they are questioning during your discussion with them. Opportunities can also arise by listening for "triggers" to get hints about their lifestyle and specific needs. As a salesperson, if you remain observant and always listen for "triggers", your opportunities will increase significantly.

Occasionally, however, you may find that the customer is "on a mission", either pushed for time and wants to complete their shopping as soon as possible, or knows exactly what they want and again, wants to make their purchase quickly. In these instances, often, the customer cannot be swayed no matter how hard you try, by value-add, up-selling or cross-selling.

Making the Transition from the Initial Enquiry

Before making the transition to value-add, up-sell or cross-sell, you will need to refer back to previous conversation with the customer, working out if it's appropriate to do it.

Asking yourself things like:

"Is there is a feeling that this could work"

"Are they in too much of a hurry?"

"Do they trust me?"

are all key elements to deciding if it is an appropriate action to take in the particular selling situation you are in. Once you have decided to proceed, transitioning to value-add, up-selling or cross-selling should be smooth and seamless. Value-add selling is usually carried out after closing the initial sale, whilst up-selling and cross-selling are usually done prior to the initial closure.

As discussed previously, picking up on "triggers" is one of the best ways to transition into these additional selling methods. This is your opportunity to introduce the customer to complimentary or additional products that they may also buy; similar products of a higher price bracket, or slightly different products that may better suit their needs. To ensure the transition from the initial enquiry is seamless, be sure to mention the particular "trigger" that you are acting on during the transition.

For example, in previous conversation, your customer mentioned that he/she had children. If this is the trigger that you will use to value-add, up-sell or cross-sell, be sure to relate your sales pitch directly to how the children can benefit.

An example of a transition to value-add selling is:

"You mentioned that you had children. Have you seen our range of educational software that could suit them? It connects easily to the system that you are buying today..........."

Single Price Point Selling

Single Price Point Selling (SPPS) is selling a combination of your products or your services based on one, single price point. For example, you may sell 3 t-shirts for a single price, or offer a free small screen tv with the purchase of a larger one. The accent is on the single or final price, not the prices of the individual items. Usually, this is prearranged or preset as a package-type offer, and often represents a significant discount for the customer.

Your store may have many offers like this. Your responsibility as a salesperson is to understand the single price point selling concept, and sell packages like this as they are designed to be sold, not break them up into individual items.

If you are offering single price point goods, you need to draw your customer's attention to the savings that can be made on such offers, which will often encourage them to buy. If you can show them examples of similar items at individual prices which will end up costing them more, then the single price point goods will usually win them over.

Some examples of single price point selling are:

- 2 t-shirts for $35.00, when the same t-shirt individually sells for $19.95   *saving of $4.90*

- A cup of coffee and a muffin for $5.00, when individually, these items would add up to $7.40 *saving of $2.40*

- A vacuum cleaner with a bonus handyvac for $110.00, when the items are priced at $99.00 and $39.00 respectively when purchased separately *saving of $28.00*

Why Do We Use Single Price Point Selling?

Single price point selling isn't always only about saving the customer money. SPPS can be very useful when selling and will usually benefit both the store and the customer, significantly. The key reasons for using SPPS are:

- Volume sales of stock
- Helps move slower selling items
- Saves the customer money
- Makes shopping easy for the customer
- Saves the customer time

VOLUME SALES

Single price point selling is most often used to generate *volume sales*. (We looked at these previously in *Chapter 9*). This could be for items of stock that are in plentiful supply and need to be moved, or items which carry good rebates from the manufacturers and which will greatly benefit the store if sales in large volumes are recorded.

Sometimes the items packaged up in a SPP deal will have a lower profit margin than if those same items were sold separately, but the sheer volume of the sales more than makes up for the shortfall in the profit margin, as a far greater number of that item is sold. This increase in volume is usually due to the fact that most SPP packages offer significant savings to the customer, so more sales are made of those items in the package deal than would usually be made if those items were sold individually.

SLOW MOVERS

Single price point selling is also an effective way of moving items that have proved to be slow or poor sellers. Often, slow moving items are packaged together with items of a similar nature at a greatly reduced price, or piggy-backed with a good selling item to help bring stock levels of the slow movers down.

SAVES CUSTOMER MONEY

SPPS more often than not offers significant savings to the customer, by offering items at a lower price than if those same items were purchased separately. This encourages the customer to buy. Provided that the customer has a genuine use for the items included in a SPP deal, then it is a very persuasive selling tool. If using SPPS, it is usually a good idea to give your customer the breakdown of the individual item costs, to show them what they are saving by taking up the single price point offer.

MAKES SHOPPING EASY

When offering several items as a single price point, it can also make shopping easier for the customer, as they do not have to put too much thought into the purchase – especially if they are buying items that they are not familiar with or understand how to use. This is particularly true in the case of some electrical products, where the customer may not understand exactly what they need to buy in order to get the result that they want, and may not be familiar with the technology involved.

For example, if a customer wanted to upgrade their old tv to a new home theatre system, they may not have enough technical knowledge to know exactly what to buy to achieve this. A predefined home theatre package offered as a single price point would make this task much easier for the customer and eliminate a lot of stress, as generally, the most appropriate items required would be preselected to make up the package.

SAVES CUSTOMER TIME

Single price point selling not only makes shopping easier and saves the customer money, it also saves the customer time. In the example above with the home theatre package, having the required items already offered in a single price package would not only make the shopping process easier for the customer, but would save them considerable time.

Similarly, a lady could be interested in trying some cosmetics for the first time and be overwhelmed at the choices available. She may also be unsure if a particular brand will be suitable for her skin type. A 'starter kit' of the most popular and most appropriate items in a particular range, offered as a cost effective single price point item, would be a most attractive offer to the customer in this instance. Not only will she be able to test run a variety of the products in that particular range, but by buying the products in the SPP kit, she will be saving money and valuable time.

Positive Pitching

Positive pitching is a process or technique used to put a positive slant on a negative situation, to turn it around and make it look like a positive. Positive pitching involves using positive words in your language and gestures such as smiling, nodding and appropriate hand gestures. Your body language should also be open and positive. (Refer back to *Chapter 6 – Behaviour & Body Language* if you need to reacquaint yourself with these concepts).

Positive pitching during the sales process can involve using examples of feedback from other happy customers. Some examples are things like:

"Our feedback on this item has been great"

To date, we haven't had one complaint or product return on this"............"

"Reviews of this product has been excellent"

Remember, however, positive pitching will only work if you have belief in your products and services. You must ensure that you have adequate product knowledge and confidence in the product or service that you are selling.

The Benefits of Positive Pitching

Positive pitching is a useful selling tool and can bring about benefits for both you and the business. It will help your customer feel more comfortable about their purchase, and, as a result, will often help you up-sell and cross-sell. You must ensure, however, that your 'pitch' is genuine. You need to have good product knowledge about what you are selling, and a genuine belief in the product yourself. It is no good trying to convince a customer to buy something that is clearly not suitable or of no interest to them, no matter how much of a positive slant you can generate. Similarly, being dishonest or outright lying about the merits of a product that is in truth not what you say it is, is not an example of positive pitching. As we have seen in other chapters, this type of behaviour will only undermine your credibility as a salesperson, and will not benefit you in the long run.

Positive pitching is helpful in reinforcing the merits of a product or service to a customer, and may sometimes be the catalyst that initiates the switch in their head, convincing them to buy. It is a powerful sales tool that can be used to increase your sales potential.

You might use positive pitching to:

- help move excess stock
- move stock that provides a greater margin or rebate for the business
- move stock that management have specifically requested you to try to move
- sell stock that is an advertised line
- or simply to move product that is great value and will lead to further good feedback and customer referrals

Don't confuse or overwhelm your customer, however, with trying to utilise all these additional selling techniques in one conversation. Judge the situation and select those which are most appropriate and likely to give the best result!

"You must not only aim right, but draw the bow with all your might."

<u>Henry David Thoreau</u> – American author, poet & philosopher

---

Key Factors for Success

When using additional selling methods like value-add selling, up-selling, cross-selling, single price point selling or positive pitching, the main things to remember are:

❖ Be as certain as you can that it is an appropriate action to take in the first place

❖ Take the time to physically show the customer items that compliment or enhance their purchase *and* how they do so

❖ Give your customer a breakdown of the individual costs of items in a SPP package to show them exactly what they are saving or how they benefit

❖ If selling a service, explain clearly what you are offering in addition or instead and ensure that your customer understands

❖ Don't push too hard if you can see that the customer is not interested or cannot be swayed

❖ When using positive pitching, ensure that you maintain your honesty about the product or service that you are selling. Don't make outrageous claims that are clearly untrue just to make the product or service appear better than it really is.

---

18. POINT OF SALE (POS)

"It's not the employer who pays the wages. Employers only handle the money. It's the customer who pays the wages."

<u>Henry Ford</u> - American founder of the Ford Motor Company

What is POS?

Point of sale or *POS* is the term used to describe the devices used to record transactions in a store – generally sales. It is the modern day 'cash register' and is based on a computer system, 'though the actual styles are many and varied. The point of sale might be at a checkout - as in a supermarket – or situated on a counter, as most retail stores tend to do. There might be just one point of sale in a store, or several, as in a department store.

All POS systems look different. Although the basic composition is the same, systems will vary greatly, depending on the environment it is being used in; the type of information that is required to be gathered or recorded; the type of look the store is after and, of course, the amount of money a store wants to spend on the set up. Systems will range from a very basic cash register-looking type, through to more complex, high-end systems with touch screen facilities instead of keyboards.

The basic configuration of a POS system is explained below, where the fundamental components that make up most POS systems are listed and their functions explained in basic terms.

Computer	Performs all the processes and stores data in memory
Screen	Displays data so it can be read by the operator
Keyboard	Enables the entry of data into the computer system and activates various functions
Mouse	Enables an alternate way of entering data into the computer and assists in activating functions
Cash drawer	Houses the float and provides a secure place to collect and store money, cheques and EFTPOS slips
Scanner (barcode scanner)	This 'reads' the barcodes on the products and 'feeds' the information about the product into the computer
Docket printer	Prints a record of the transaction performed
EFTPOS machine	Enables a credit card payment by a customer to be processed

The function of the point of sale in a retail store, is to process transactions and collect and record raw data about that transaction. A transaction can be a sale, a refund, to generate or redeem a credit note or a gift voucher, to process a lay-by, or simply to record a customer's details in the store's data base.

The data that is collected at the point of sale is usually about the item or items being sold/returned. Often, most of this data will be automatically generated by the computer after scanning the barcode, (we will look at this in more detail a little later), or it may be keyed in or entered in manually by the person operating the POS. Some of the pieces of information that are collected by a POS system during a transaction are as follows. There are often also many more.

- Item code
- Item description
- Colour of item
- Size
- Quantity of items purchased
- Price(s) of items
- Date of transaction
- Type of transaction
- Customer's details
- Method of payment
- Any discounts applied
- Loyalty points earned (if applicable)

Understanding Your Store POS

As we have seen, raw data relating to a transaction is collected by the POS system at the store. This data is then converted to information for the store to analyse and use later, and is stored in the computer's memory. If the store is part of a chain and reports to a head office, the information is relayed to an integrated computer system at the head office and stored there. The information that is collected from the store allows head office (or the store owner) to make strategic and vision-based decisions such as financial planning for the future.

Decisions on stock selection - i.e. what items are selling well and what items aren't; what sizes or colours of particular items are the most popular; what sort of quantities of popular items are required to meet customer demands etc – can help a store plan ahead to better meet demands and reduce mistakes in buying. Decisions about how many stores are viable to operate; how many staff are needed and which staff are the best or worst performers, can all be determined from information collected at point of sale and analysed in reports.

This is why it is very important a salesperson, to ensure that you are recording the correct information in each transaction that you perform. Incorrect data can paint a different picture about what is happening at store level, and can affect the outcome of some high level decisions. Ensuring that you are giving the store owner or your head office the correct information to work with, will lead to improvements at the store which will benefit you as well. If the stock selection is improved, your opportunities to make sales also increase.

POS Security & Help

POS systems are usually protected, to a degree, from fraudulent use by way of login codes for staff to use, and different levels of authorisation to allow or disallow a staff member to perform a particular function. For example, you may find that you are unable to perform a refund or open the cash drawer without a sale, unless a senior member logs in to take over. Restrictions may also be in place to authorise things like issuing gift vouchers or credit notes.

You should also be aware of who to call or report problems with your POS system to, when they occur. From time to time, you will experience a variety of issues or problems with the system 'going down' or 'freezing' and it's important to know who your point of contact is for computer support. Ask your manager or other team members if you are not sure.

Incorporating Your POS system & Your Customer

The process of carrying out the sale (or other) transaction at the point of sale should be quick and easy for the customer. Now that they have made their decision on what to buy, chances are, they just want to pay for it and leave. Even small delays during the transaction process can seem to be very long for a customer, who may have many other things to go and do, or somewhere else that they need to be.

Depending on the type of POS system that your store has, the sale process may involve a few steps and will require you to concentrate on what you are doing. It is not a good idea, however, to just put your head down and perform these steps, forgetting about your customer who is standing in front of you. It is very important to maintain eye contact and continue to communicate with the customer throughout the sales process. Remember, a good rule of thumb is to treat customers the way that you would like to be treated if you were in their shoes. No-one likes to be ignored, so ensure that you keep up the same friendly service and polite manner that you would have exhibited throughout the entire sales process when you are at the point of sale.

Opportunities at Point of Sale

The point of sale can also be a good place try and capitalise on other sales opportunities like those we looked at in the last chapter, Chapter 17 – Additional Selling Techniques. If you haven't already done so during the sales process, the point of sale can be a great place to value-add to your sale, while you still have your customer in the store. For example, if you are selling clothing, you can use the opportunity at point of sale to see if the customer is interested in also buying accessories like a belt, jewellery, tie, scarf, gloves etc. You could tell them about upcoming sales or special promotions that the store may be having soon, or ask them if they'd like to join your VIP club or loyalty program. You may want to let them know about your store's website and how they can keep up to date with what's happening in your store or ask them questions about their experience today as a customer.

The opportunities to build rapport with your customer at the point of sale are many, and taking the extra time to communicate with your customer in this way, can often lead to added rewards for you as a salesperson. Not only do you have the opportunity to increase your sale with value-add items, but you are continuing to build a relationship with that customer, which will lead to advantages in the future.

POS Components in Detail

At the beginning of this chapter, we touched on the basic components of a typical point of sale system that you might find in a retail store. Following is a more detailed list of components that make up a POS system and a more detailed explanation of how they work. You might find this helpful to refer to from time to time.

"If you put good people in bad systems you get bad results. You have to water the flowers you want to grow."

Stephen R Covey – American author

COMPONENT	DETAILED DESCRIPTION OF WORKINGS
Computer	Often confused with the screen, the computer is actually the 'box' part of the system, containing all the memory and the processing components. It has a power button to turn the entire system on or off and has cables leading from it to link up with the other components in the system. It is usually kept under the counter and should have good ventilation at all times as it can get quite hot during use. Sometimes the computer is actually built into the screen if the system is a "touch-screen" system. The computer should *never* be opened by anyone other than qualified IT personnel who are usually specially employed by the store to maintain and service the POS systems.
Screen	This displays the information that is being generated by the computer, so the operator can see what function to perform next. It interacts with the keyboard and/or mouse to display what is typed in or entered. Screens can also be a "touch screen" variety which is operated by touching "hot spots" or special sensitive areas on the screen with your finger, indicated by a picture or "icon" to activate a particular function. Keyboards are usually not required in a touch screen system. All screens should be kept clean, free of dust and grease. This is particularly important for touch screens.
Keyboard	Used to input information to the system. The traditional keyboard is known as a *"qwerty"* keyboard, referring to the first six letters on the top row. Some specialist keyboards can be programmed so that hitting certain keys immediately performs a specific function.

Mouse	This is a hand operated device used to move the "cursor" to a specific point on the screen. It is often quicker and easier to navigate around a screen using a mouse, however, in most POS systems, the software is designed so that the operator can also make quick selections on the screen using the keyboard.
Software	This is the program or set of instructions that the computer system uses to carry out particular functions. Software for point of sale systems can range from fairly basic varieties to carry out sales, refunds, lay-bys, redeem gift vouches or credit notes and generate very simple reports on sales figures, to complex versions that can cater for stocktakes and multiple store operations and are capable of generating very detailed reports to outline top and bottom sellers, stock movement, profit and loss, cash flow etc
Cash drawer	These come in many different sizes or styles depending on the environment you are in. The one you use might be under the counter and pops out/open at the completion of a sale, or your store might have one with a flip-top lid like in some supermarkets. Some are fitted with a timer for added security. At the start or end of a shift, you may be required to carry a cash drawer from the office to your till or vice versa. Your cash drawer should be regularly cleared to minimise the amount of cash kept on the shop floor in case of theft.
Barcode scanner	Used to "read" barcode labels, barcode scanners can be either mounted onto the counter, hand-held, or set below the counter so that items are passed across it to be read – like

	in many supermarkets now. The scanner has a red laser or diode that scans a barcode for information. The scanner is simply waved over the barcode so that the laser light lines up with the barcode label on the product. Some scanners have cables attached and some are wireless. Some have buttons to press or a trigger to activate the laser. The information contained in the barcode is linked to a database in the software and once read by the laser, this information is displayed on the screen.
Docket printer	These too, can be many and varied in style and mode of operation, but all perform the same function – to provide a printed record of the transaction performed. Different styles of docket printers will use different consumables. Some use ribbons and some don't. Some use specially treated thermal paper and some use plain. Docket printers must be kept clean of dust and lint and it is vital to install replacement consumables correctly so as not to cause damage to the machine.
EFTPOS unit	Similarly to a docket printer, EFTPOS units vary in design and operation and use different types of consumables. The function of the EFTPOS unit is to directly connect the system to the customer's bank through the phone line, so a credit card or EFTPOS card can be debited. Cards are generally swiped through the reader section or inserted into the machine so that the customer's account details can be read. Some newer styles like the IP EFTPOS unit are connected to the banks via the internet instead of the phone line. If the internet goes down, these new units have a 3G connection to allow them to keep processing.

Customer displays	Older styles of POS often had customer display poles attached with green LED lights to display some of the information that the operator sees on their screen to the customer. This allowed the customer to see things like the price and quantity of the items that they were being charged for, as well as the total cost and method of payment. Now it is more common to see full size screens complete with a full list of all products being purchased, along with prices AND pictures. Sometimes this display will also feature advertising. As these displays face the customer, they should be kept clean and operating correctly at all times.
Virus protection	Along with the operating and POS software, a system must have virus protection software to ensure valuable data is not corrupted or lost. This is of vital importance if data is being transferred to a head office, so that their system is not infected or corrupted. There are many different types of virus protection software packages that are commonly used. They usually have an expiry date and must be regularly renewed in order for them to remain effective. A warning is normally displayed as an expiry date is approaching or if the software has already expired.
UPS (uninterrupted power supply)	A device that the computer plugs into as well as the normal power outlet, to protect it in times of disruption to the power supply or when there are spikes & power surges, which can damage electrical equipment like computers. Having the UPS take over from the power supply if it is cut, also allows the computer to shut down correctly before it crashes, when it is vulnerable to losing data.

Multi-POS stations	Bigger stores and department stores will have many point of sale areas, each with their own POS system and cash drawer etc, but are all linked by the POS software so that they all access and record to the same database. Each station needs to be cashed up and reconciled independently and is usually identified by a number or letter. If you are working in a multi-station environment, it is important to make sure that you are logging on correctly so that all the data from any transactions conducted is collected and recorded in the correct way.

CARLO G SANTORO

19. PHONE CALLS, EMAILS & INTERNET SALES

"If you do build a great experience, customers tell each other about that. Word of mouth is very powerful."

Jeff Bezos – Founder of the popular online book store: Amazon.com.

Prompt Answering

As a retail salesperson, you will be expected to both make and take calls to and from customers. When taking a call from a customer, you must ensure that you answer promptly – usually within three rings. A customer does not like sitting on the phone for too long. They are expecting to have their call answered and their needs met promptly. Taking too long to answer a call can signify to a customer that your store is not interested in taking their call or in helping them. Also, if you fail to answer a call from your customers promptly, you may miss out on business. Customers may be calling you with a sales enquiry. If you fail to answer the customers' calls, you may miss out on their sales enquiry and the opportunity to make a sale.

Taking Customer Calls When Serving

Just as it is important to answer customer calls promptly, it is also vitally important not to give the incoming call priority over a customer who is actually in the store that may require your attention. The customer in front of you in the store is always more important than answering the phone.

Answering a call while you are in the midst of a conversation with a customer in the store, or when they are just about to ask for assistance, can be disastrous. Your in-store customer is likely to walk out or at the very least become annoyed, which may cause you to not only lose the potential sale, but lose them as a customer in the future as well. How to handle this situation – particularly if you are the only salesperson on the floor - can seem tricky, however, it can be dealt with easily and with positive results all round, if handled the correct way.

If you are the only salesperson on the floor and must handle both the in-store customer and the incoming call, the best way to do so is to politely excuse yourself from your in-store customer and answer the call promptly - apologising and explaining to the caller that you are with another customer and that you will be more than happy to call them back shortly, if they'd like to leave their details. When returning to your in-store customer, apologise for the disruption and resume helping them. Dealing with the situation in this way, you will minimise any disservice to either of the customers.

Professional Greeting

When greeting a customer over the phone, you must ensure that you are clear and professional. You should never answer with just "hello", the way you would answer your personal phone. Your company may have a set greeting to use that is company policy, but if not, as a good rule of thumb, always say your business' name and your name.

A professional greeting can be done in many different ways. No matter how you greet your customers, you must always ensure that you are professional, polite and friendly, even if you are busy, tired or stressed. It is important that you always impart positive messages about your business to the customer on the end of the phone. A professional greeting helps to ensure that the customer will feel confident in dealing with you and your store.

Some examples of professional greetings are:

"Good afternoon, Downtown Supermarket. You're speaking with James...."

"Richard's Menswear. My name is Paul. How can I help you?"

"Good morning, Blondie's Boutique. This is Melanie..."

What Your Customer Hears

Your customers can hear a lot more over the phone than you realise. Your tone of voice will say a lot about you as a salesperson as well as your attitude and willingness to assist your customer with their enquiry. Your tone of voice can be determined by things such as mood, attitude, body language and posture. Your customers can also hear whether or not you are smiling. Believe it or not, this is true!

Your mood and attitude will help determine your tone of voice. A person in a happy cheerful mood, with a positive attitude, will display a positive and energetic tone of voice. This will assist the customer to feel welcome and to feel as if you are genuinely willing to assist them with their enquiry. A salesperson in a cheerful mood with positive attitude is also more likely to take a pro-active approach to selling and therefore achieve a more positive outcome.

Body language and posture will also help determine your tone of voice, as well as your attitude. If you are sitting or leaning in a lazy position with a dismal look on your face, you are more likely to display a lazy and ambivalent attitude to your customers. However, if you are standing up tall with a smile on your face, your customers will hear a cheerful person with a positive attitude. This is the type of person your customer wants to do business with.

Using the right intonation in your sentences will also display a more positive attitude to your customers. Making the words at the end of your sentences go 'up' instead of down will show that you are feeling more positive and they can hear this in the tone of your voice.

Speaking slightly louder than you would in a face to face situation is also something to remember when speaking on the phone. Bad lines and background noise can interfere with your conversation and make it difficult for your customer to fully grasp what you are saying. Using a slightly louder voice will also dictate a subtle authority in what you are saying, giving you more confidence in what you are trying to sell or resolve with the customer.

Remember too, when listening to a customer speaking - especially if they are telling you something long and involved - ensure that you indicate that you are listening intently. Interject here and there with words like: "*Oh yes*", "*OK*" and "*Of course*", to show that you are following what they are saying to you.

Explaining Products & Services Clearly

When you are on the phone to a customer who is making a sales enquiry, you must ensure that you explain all the products and services that you are discussing very clearly. Unlike being in a retail outlet, your customers cannot see you or the products that you are referring to. The only way to know exactly what product or service is on offer is to listen to and interpret what you are saying. This is why you must explain everything slowly and extremely clearly. If a customer is confused by what you are offering, they may present you with objections, or simply hang up no longer interested.

When explaining, enunciate your words carefully and don't mumble. You might know the product backwards, but it could be the first time that the customer is hearing about it and they may not understand everything straight away. If you are explaining how something works, keep the technical jargon to a minimum and use words that the customer will understand.

It's also a good idea to pretend sometimes that you are a customer in a phone conversation with a salesperson and think about the sorts of things you would like to hear and the way you would like them to be said.

Making Customer Calls

Similarly to taking customer calls, at times, your role as a sales person will involve making outbound calls to customers. This may be because you were unable to take their initial call as you were busy serving an in-store customer, or for other reasons. If you are returning a customer's call because you were busy previously, ensure that you call them back as soon as you possibly can and apologise for the delay. You might be amazed at the reaction. All too often, customers are left with empty promises of a call back that never comes. Ensuring that you follow through, your efforts will be very welcomed by the recipient, making it easier to handle the request they may have asked for.

Other reasons that you may need to make an outbound call to a customer are to make follow-up calls, update them with information relating to a previous conversation or correspondence, or to confirm appointments. We will look at each of these now:

FOLLOW-UP CALLS

There will be times where you may be required to make a follow-up call (or email). This may be when your customer has presented you with an objection and you are contacting them to relay new information or answer questions that they may have raised, or it may be after you have been sent correspondence about promotions or deals that you are offering and you would like to let your customers know. To ensure that your customer has not forgotten about your products or services, you will need to take the initiative to make a follow-up call or email.

A suitable timeframe for a follow-up call or email is usually around one week unless otherwise stated. If you have made an appointment time to make a follow-up call, you must ensure that you stick to the time and date that you had previously organised with your customer in order be seen as trustworthy and dependable. A failure to adhere to prior arrangements could deem you as irresponsible and unprofessional.

RELATING TO PREVIOUS CORRESPONDENCE & CONVERSATION

It is important when you are making a follow-up call or email, that you relate your conversation to previous correspondence or a previous conversation. This will show your customer that you are not just another salesperson "cold calling", but that you have made previous contact with them. For example, you may have sent out a letter to your customer about a special promotion that you have on offer. When you make a follow-up call, be sure to mention the letter you sent as it shows your customer that you are not a "cold caller".

You may find too, that in your absence on a particular day, another team member may have also assisted the customer that you were originally helping with an issue. Any resolutions to their initial problem or a progress report should be noted down in the customer file or CRM (customer relationship management system) It is important to refer to these notes before contacting your customer to ensure that you are not wasting time going over things that may have already been handled or resolved. Keeping these notes up to date and accurate is also vital to make it easy for anyone else to follow how the situation has been handled to date.

CONFIRMING APPOINTMENTS

There may be times when you are required to confirm appointments with you customers. If you have booked an appointment, you must ensure that you confirm the appointment time the day before. If there is a long period of time between the booking of the appointment and the appointment date, you may be required to send a reminder email or letter, as well as make the call one day prior. The reminder email should be sent about half way between the booking date and the appointment date.

When making the reminder call or sending the reminder correspondence to your customer, be sure to advise them of any cancellation or missed appointment charges that may be applicable if they were to miss their scheduled appointment, so that they are fully aware of any financial consequences if they fail to turn up.

Ending the Call

When ending a call with a customer, you must show that you will be willing to also assist them in future. This is done by asking if there is anything else they need assistance with, advising that you are available to assist with any further enquiries and thanking your customer for their call. Just because your current call is ending, does not mean that there will be no further interaction with that customer later down the track. It is also important that you reiterate the question or problem that they originally posed to you. Ask them if you've succeeded in helping them or resolved their issue. If there were multiple issues, run through the list to see if you've covered everything.

Some examples of closing lines could be:

"I'm glad that I was able to help you. Is there anything that I can do for you?"

"Thank you very much for your call. Have I answered all your questions today?"

"It was a pleasure. Happy to help. Have I solved the problem for you now?"

Transferring a Call

If you find that you are not able to assist a customer with their problem or issue, don't just pass them straight onto someone else or put them on hold for another team member or department to pick up. This will reflect badly on your professionalism and will not be a nice experience for the customer. If you need to pass them onto someone else, ensure that you give a *'warm transfer'* or introduction to the person or department that will be assisting them. This ensures that they are aware of the problem and do not have to ask the customer to repeat everything, and is also a nicer way for you to transfer your customer's call on.

Some examples of warm transfers could be:

"Mr Jones, I'm just going to put you through to Sharon in our service department and she'll be able to assist you further. I'll transfer you now…."

"Marion, I have Mrs Winston on the line. She needs your help with an account query. Mrs Winston, I'll give you to Marion now to look up that transaction for you....."

Internet Sales

With the popularity of online stores and customers buying directly over the internet, shopping for some customers has changed considerably. Some people will happily seek out the items that they require and use the virtual 'checkout' to pay for them and give their delivery details. All this can be done without any human intervention and therefore without any 'customer service' as we know it. An online retailer must still ensure that their customers have a positive experience when making their purchases, to ensure that they come back in the future. They do this by making their websites easy to navigate around and ensure that the purchasing procedure is quick and secure.

Some customers, however, are still nervous about using the internet to purchase goods and are dubious about the security of e-commerce. They may prefer to phone up and speak to someone about the procedure before they go ahead. Some online stores do provide a number where customers can contact a service representative, but many online stores do not. If your store has an online store operating on its website, you may find that you receive calls from customers who want to ask about a product or a return, or verify the security measures in place to safeguard the transfer of funds etc.

As a salesperson, you may need to know the answers to these sorts of questions and know how these processes on the website work. As internet sales is a fast-growing area in retail, you might also find that your particular store may be one designated from the chain to take all the internet sale phone calls for enquiries on the internet side of the business, making it imperative that you are able to answer all the questions that customers may ask you.

The customers that you speak to and assist may still end up buying their goods online, and not from you personally, but by answering any questions that they may call you about, you can help them feel at ease and comfortable about proceeding. Some other customers too, may use the store to look at a product, pick it up, try it on etc and then still buy online at another time. You need to be aware of all these factors associated with internet sales as they are definitely here to stay.

Particular Care with Emails

When using email as the method of correspondence, whether it is associated with an internet sale from an online store, or as the chosen method of correspondence for contacting a customer form your store, particular care must be taken to ensure that the correct tone is portrayed.

Unlike a phone conversation, the customer receiving the email cannot hear you. They cannot hear your tone of voice, attitude, body language, whether or not you are smiling etc. All those important factors relating to phone manner, which can directly impact on your sales outcome, are conveyed to the customer in one go – in your email. And in 99% of cases, once an email is sent, it is irretrievable.

If the wrong message is conveyed, or the customer interprets an unfriendly, unprofessional or condescending tone in your email, any hope of maintaining a good rapport with that customer may be lost. Worse still, if an email was deemed to be particularly offensive or inappropriate to a customer, it could cost you your job.

"There's no ceiling on effort!"

Harvey C. Fruehauf - Founding investor in Burger King

Checklist for Sending Emails

❖ Always keep your emails *to the point* – don't waffle on too much.

❖ Use a *friendly but professional greeting* like: Dear Sir, Dear Mrs X etc.

❖ *Always* ensure that the information you have included in your email is *correct*– i.e. correct item, correct price(s), correct date and/or time etc.

❖ *Make sure* that what you are telling the customer in your email has been *verified* as correct by a senior staff member – i.e. don't tell a customer that they can return their purchase for a refund if that is not the case.

❖ *Always* spell check your words before sending the email. A badly worded or misspelled email conveys a strong sense of unprofessionalism and a "no care" attitude. This is not what you want to convey to your customers.

❖ Use a *friendly but professional ending* like: Yours sincerely…., Thanking you…., Respectfully yours…

❖ Add your *name and contact details* in case the customer needs to contact you again in the future

CARLO G SANTORO

20. COMPLAINTS HANDLING & STORE SECURITY

"When people talk about successful retailers and those that are not so successful, the customer determines at the end of the day who is successful and for what reason."

<u>Gerry Harvey</u> - Front man of the successful Australian retailing chain: Harvey Norman

Customer Service Complaints

When working in retail, as with any customer service environment, there will be times when you receive complaints about the level of customer service that a customer feels that they have experienced. These complaints might be directly face to face by a current or recent customer, or over the phone, via email, fax or letter. Some complaints may be delivered directly to you by your manager following a complaint that they have received.

There are different ways to handle customer service complaints, depending on how they are received. If you are face to face with a customer in the store, the best way to deal with the situation is to move them away from other customers to a quieter area of the store, and listen carefully to what they have to say. It is very important that you let them vocalise their issues without you interrupting. This is a prime example of when you should use your active listening skills. As we looked at in an earlier chapter, active listening shows your customer respect, and will also enable you to correctly interpret all the information that they are giving you, helping you to decipher the correct solution.

The same active listening skills should be performed if the customer complaint is via the phone. Again, as we have looked at previously, as the customer cannot see you, whilst letting the customer vent their anger without interruption, ensure that you are showing them that you are listening to them and hearing everything that they are saying (you might remember that this is done by interjecting here and there with words like: "*Oh yes*", "*OK*" and "*Of course*" to show that you are following what they are saying to you).

Actioning Complaints

After listening intently to what your customer has to say, it is important for you to identify and understand exactly what the key issue is to deal with. During your customer's delivery of their complaint, because they may have been upset, they could have included a lot of irrelevant details masking what the actual problem is that they are complaining about. Sometimes it's a good idea to briefly reiterate what you understand the exact nature of their problem to be, to ensure that you have interpreted all the facts correctly.

If the customer asks to see the manager, you will need to contact them immediately and advise them of the situation – preferably away from the customer's range of hearing. Ideally, after discussing the challenge with your manager, you may have come up with a solution which will enable you to rectify the situation with the customer, without the manager actively getting involved any further. Sometimes, if a manager gets directly involved in a situation like this too early, it can make it difficult for them to make a decision on how to handle the problem as they may not have all the facts at that point in time.

If you are dealing with a customer service complaint face to face or over the phone, it is often a good idea to recommend that the customer put the complaint in writing – either by email, letter or fax. They may also be directed to the company's corporate website, where they can either fill out a form or email directly, to have their complaint go directly to a head office or customer service division. When dealing with all customer complaints, always get the customer's name and some details regarding their issue. You can then get back to them with a solution or ask your manager to contact them to sort it out.

Remember, the goal with any customer service complaint is to sort out the issue and help the customer, not make them more angry. Working through issues like these, a business will learn ways to improve their services and help their customers more.

Product Complaints

There will be many occasions that you will encounter where a customer will have a complaint about a product which they have purchased, and will want to return it for an exchange or refund.

Every company has its own set of terms and conditions surrounding product returns and you should make sure that you are fully aware of exactly what these are for your store. Product returns for a change of mind, an unwanted gift or incorrect purchase etc will often differ, however, from those where the product has proven to be faulty. When a product is faulty, the customer is normally entitled to a repair, a replacement or sometimes a refund, even though they may not fulfill the normal requirements for a return

For example, your store's policy on returns for a change of mind or unwanted gift may be that as long as the goods are in the same condition as when they were purchased, the return is being made within a designated time frame, and the goods are accompanied by the original receipt/proof of purchase, an exchange or refund will be issued. With the case of a faulty item, however, the customer could have had the item and used it for some time and may no longer have the receipt.

With electrical or motorised products, it is essential that you fully understand the warranty conditions that are associated with each product in case they break down or malfunction and are returned to your store. You need to know that in the case of a faulty item being returned by a customer, is it your company's or the manufacturer who is actually responsible? If you are not sure, ask your manger to explain what the warranty covers and how you could help a customer get a faulty product serviced or replaced, if need be. The main concern ultimately, is to service the customer who is likely to be very unhappy.

Government Regulations

In any region, you will find that there will always be certain laws or government regulations that affect all product and service-based businesses like retail stores. These regulations are to protect consumers from being caught out with faulty goods that a retailer or manufacturer may try to avoid taking responsibility for.

When setting your store's terms and conditions, your head office will ensure that they abide by the government regulations that cover the products that you sell or services that you offer. You should be aware of what these government rulings are and understand how they affect the way that you service your customer. If you are not sure about these, ask your manager for a copy of any regulations that are applicable to your business, or a high level overview of consumer rights. You may also benefit from some training in this area to ensure that you are familiar with what is law in your region.

Logging Complaints

Complaints of any nature should always be logged to ensure that the store has an accurate record of the complaint and who it is from. Your store may use a special book, diary or form or it may be part of your regular *shift report* which is filled out at the end of each day or shift. (We looked at shift reports back in Chapter 4)

Some companies may require a store to log complaints via the corporate website or via email directly to the head office. Whatever way that your store requires you to log complaints, the information recorded would essentially be the same. You would need the customer's contact details and a full description of what the complaint is about. Logging the correct information is vital so that the right person in the business can handle it after you have dealt with it initially.

Following is an example of a customer complaint log. It is important that as well as passing the complaint onto the right person to action, that you follow up on this as well. Letting the customer know that their complaint has been taken seriously and that it has been dealt with at a higher level, will help put the customer at ease. Ensuring too that you continue to follow up on the progress of the resolution and reporting this to the customer, would be very good customer service on your part.

Customer Complain Log:

Date	Saturday, 4th March 2009
Store location	Melbourne Central
Staff member reporting complaint	Audrey Williams
Customer's name	Elsie Min
Customer's address	52 Elwood Road Carnegie Vic 3054
Customer's phone number (s)	03 9572 6754 Mobile: 0423 786 917
Customer's email address	elsiem@hotmail.com
Customer's complaint	Mrs Min phoned and asked for a copy of a best-selling book to be put on hold as it was the last copy in the store. She said she'd be down at lunch time to collect it. When she arrived, she found that the sales person hadn't put the copy aside for her and someone else had bought it. She was very upset as she drove to the store especially to collect it.
Manager complaint referred onto	Harry Valencia

Understanding Store Security Systems & Devices

Most retail stores have some type of security device in place. Some even employ the services of a security guard to patrol the entrance or exit whilst the store is trading. One of the most often used devices, however, is a security camera or closed circuit tv system. One of the primary reasons why security cameras are installed into stores is to ensure the

84

safety of the staff. Companies must ensure that your safety is maintained at all times and security cameras provide a way of monitoring all areas of the store throughout the trading period in addition to whilst it is closed. Another reason to monitor the store is to deter theft or capture the act on tape to aid in the prosecution of the offenders. If a product is stolen or willfully damaged by a customer, the use of security cameras ensure that it is caught on video so that a store's head office can deal with the situation either through the police or centre management, if the store is located in a shopping mall. Security cameras and any associated devices should not be tampered with, and are usually left alone to do their job once they are set up.

Security cameras normally run 24/7 around the clock, and do not just capture what the customers are doing, but they are also used to monitor the staff. You should be aware that in the course of a normal day in your store you may very well be being watched – but for several different reasons. Some companies will monitor footage from security cameras to see how you work; where you walk in the store; how the customers are being attended to etc. Others will use the cameras to ensure that their staff are not acting in a manner that breaches the store's behaviour code or employment agreement or worse still, that they are not stealing money or merchandise.

Fashion stores and some stores selling electrical goods have special devices attached to the products which set off loud beeping alarms located at the exit of the store if the goods pass through the exit and they are not part of a legitimate sale. These security devices must be disconnected or removed by the salesperson at the time of purchase to prevent the alarms being activated. The devices are attached to the products and can only be removed by a special tool installed at the point of sale. Some customers may attempt to remove the devices in the change room or in a secluded corner of the store. Others may try things like covering them in foil in the hope that this will prevent the electronic alarm being triggered. Some devices contain a special dye which will be released if an attempt is made to remove the security tag, and cover the perpetrator's hands.

Recognising & Preventing Shoplifting

Recognising and preventing theft – known in retail as '*shoplifting*' - before it happens is an important role that you as a salesperson can play. Shoplifting badly affects a store's profitability as the goods have been paid for at purchase from the wholesaler or manufacturer, but not actually sold in the store to make a profit.

The best way to prevent shoplifting is by communicating and interacting with your customers, not staying behind the counter to allow them to go to quiet or unattended areas in the store. Eye contact is essential, and maybe smile at the same time. This will let legitimate customers know that they can approach you if they need help, while prospective shoplifters will be aware that you are watching them.

When it's quiet, it's a good idea to go around the store and check that all the items that require security tags to be attached have them in place. That way, you will help to prevent possible shoplifting of those items.

Reporting Shoplifting

If you think that you may have identified a potential shoplifter in your store, the first course of action is to try and avert the situation before anything actually happens. Letting a senior staff member or your manager know, whilst keeping an eye on the person concerned, will ensure that the person is monitored carefully – perhaps by getting more staff onto the floor. More staff members present will usually discourage the potential offender from attempting to steal.

If you actually see a shoplifter in action or are certain that shoplifting has occurred, you must report it. You would first report the incident to your manager or the most senior staff member present at the time. They would then advise your head office who may in turn contact the police and/or the centre management, if your store was inside a shopping mall.

You would need to be able to identify the person – remember what they were wearing, what they looked like, their approximate age etc. You would also need to identify the item that was stolen – the make or model, size, colour etc, or at least as much information as you can remember. If your store has security cameras, the incident should be captured on video, which will aid the police in their investigation. You might find too, that other customers present at the time may have witnessed the incident and can assist you.

Like customer complaints, incidents like shoplifting need to be logged. Your store needs an accurate record of what took place, as the police would require an official report to follow up on. It could be a repeat offender known to be acting in the area, so the more information that the police can gather, the more chance they have of apprehending that person.

Shoplifting is a serious criminal offence and goes on official police record. You should never directly accuse a customer of shoplifting, but report the incident immediately to management or better still, try and avert the situation before it happens.

"You have to do what others won't. To achieve what others don't."

Anonymous

SOME WAYS TO HELP PREVENT SHOPLIFTING
Always keep an eye on customers with particularly large bags, backpacks or covered trolleys   ➤ Items can quickly be concealed in large bags, backpacks or trolleys and taken out of the store unnoticed
Walk around the store floor regularly – even if there are only one or two customers present   ➤ Customers can easily shoplift in another area of the store if you are behind the counter or you remain at a distance from them
Be aware of and identify customers exhibiting strange behaviour   ➤ Watch for those spending too much time in one area or coming in and out often but not buying anything
Take notice of people wearing clothing with large pockets or walking through the store with a coat or similar item draped over their arm   ➤ Big pockets in an overcoat make it easy for shoplifters to drop product into and a coat or jacket draped over the arm can be used to conceal stolen goods
Watch for groups of people shopping together   ➤ Sometimes repeat shoplifters will work in a group, with one or two members distracting the sales people whilst the others steal the goods
Don't leave customers alone for too long   ➤ Ensure that your customers are well looked after and avoid giving them opportunity to shoplift
Display expensive items in a different way   ➤ Expensive items are prime targets for shoplifters. This is why you will see things like jewellery being stored under secure glass display cases or in locked cabinets. Similarly, cds are not usually kept in their cases on the shop floor – only the empty case is displayed.

ABOUT THE AUTHOR

Carlo Santoro was born and educated in Melbourne, Victoria, Australia. His business interests range from the retail industry, property market and the endless opportunities on the World Wide Web, to the commercial, political and aviation arenas.

Recognising a gap in the market some years back, Carlo facilitated the start-up of a successful company developing and managing operations and IT infrastructure for retailers – RetailCare. He maintains his role there today as Managing Director.

With more than fifteen years' experience in retail workings, Santoro spends the bulk of his time as an accomplished consultant and mentor to the retail industry. He also owns and has developed over 300 websites - many with on-line stores - and is constantly adding to this portfolio.

Carlo holds an MEI (Master of Entrepreneurship and Innovation) from Swinburne University and is recognised as one of the leading business networkers in Melbourne. Although his main focus lies with RetailCare, Carlo's extensive worldwide networks and expertise at business-to-business relationship building ensure that his business activities, like his enthusiasm for new ventures, remain dynamic.

Carlo places great importance on sharing knowledge and volunteering. He has held a prestigious leadership position for over 9 years with the Entrepreneurs' Organisation (EO) – an international non-profit organisation enabling groups of entrepreneurial business peers to meet and interact globally, growing and learning from each other along the way.

Outside of business Carlo is a dedicated father, living in Melbourne with his wife and two young children. He successfully juggles time with his many entrepreneurial ventures and time with his family.

CARLO G SANTORO

www.ingramcontent.com/pod-product-compliance
Lightning Source LLC
Chambersburg PA
CBHW051342170526
45166CB00002B/921